It's Just A Thought...
But It Could Change Your Life

Life's Little Lessons on Leadership

by

John C. Maxwell

Tulsa, Oklahoma

It's Just a Thought... But It Could Change Your Life.
ISBN 1-56292-157-6
Copyright © 1996 by John C. Maxwell
5295 Triangle Parkway
Norcross, Georgia 30092

7th Printing

Published by Honor Books, Inc.
Box 55388
Tulsa, Oklahoma 74155

Introduction

Mark Twain once said, "Take your mind out every now and then and dance on it. It is getting all caked up." It was his way of saying, "Try something new, break new ground, get out of your rut."

This is good advice for all of us. Sometimes we need something to "jolt" us out of a lifeless routine—a new thought, a different slant on a familiar subject, or a bit of wisdom from the life of someone who's "walked down that road" before we did.

The quotes that follow have been selected to inspire you to see life from a different angle. Many contain a little barb or a twist to get your attention. Some will make you laugh, and others will make you think. My hope is that they will equip you to make your world better tomorrow than it is today!

It's just a thought...but it could change your life!

John C. Maxwell

Every person who has become successful has simply formed the habit of doing things that failures disliked doing and will not do.

JOHN MAXWELL

Never let go of a dream until you're ready
to wake up and make it happen.

————◆————

It takes all the running you can do to keep in
the same place. If you want to get somewhere
else, you must run at least twice as fast as that!"

THE QUEEN OF HEARTS
IN *ALICE IN WONDERLAND*

Practice doesn't make perfect—
it makes permanent.

JOHN MAXWELL

Heart is what separates
the good from the great.

MICHAEL JORDAN

———◆———

One difference between perseverance and
obstinacy is that one often comes from a strong
will, and the other from a strong won't.

HENRY WARD BEECHER

Your attitude is either your best friend
or your worst enemy, your greatest asset
or your greatest liability.

JOHN MAXWELL

Don't just learn something from every experience; learn something positive.

ALLEN H. NEUHARTH

When you're through changing, you're through.

BRUCE BARTON

People are changed, not by coercion
or intimidation, but by example.

JOHN MAXWELL

In a small town, an old codger lived in the same house for nearly fifty years. One day he surprised everyone by moving next door. When asked why he moved, he said, "I guess it's just the gypsy in me."

It's not the mountain we conquer, but ourselves.

EDMUND HILLARY
FIRST TO CLIMB MT. EVEREST

Are you bored with life?
Maybe your expecter has expired.

JOHN MAXWELL

There are no shortcuts to
anyplace worth going.

BEVERLY SILLS

One definition of insanity is to believe that
you can keep doing what you've been doing
and get different results.

Stop trying to grow your organization.
Work on people's attitudes.
If you do that, your organization will
experience 10 percent growth overnight.

JOHN MAXWELL

It pays to plan ahead. It wasn't raining
when Noah built the ark.

———◆———

I not only use all the brains I have,
but all I can borrow.

WOODROW WILSON

Leadership determines the
direction of the company.
Organization determines the
potential of the company.
Personnel determine the
success of the company.

JOHN MAXWELL

Ideas won't keep: something
must be done about them.

ALFRED NORTH WHITEHEAD

———◆———

You've got to get up every morning
with determination if you're going
to go to bed with satisfaction.

GEORGE HORACE LORIMER

Pay now, play later;
play now, pay later.

JOHN MAXWELL

The best cure for a sluggish mind
is to disturb its routine.

WILLIAM H. DANFORTH

———◆———

He who is good at making excuses
is seldom good for anything else.

BENJAMIN FRANKLIN

We first form habits.
Then habits form us.

JOHN MAXWELL

Most people want to change the world to improve their lives. What a wasted effort. If they would only improve themselves, they would be better off and so would the world.

In youth we want to change the world.
In old age we want to change youth.

GARTH HENRICHS

People stop growing when the price gets too high.

JOHN MAXWELL

The richest soil, uncultivated,
produces the rankest weeds.

PLUTARCH

———◆———

Any time the going seems easier, better check
and see if you're not going downhill.

Image is what people think we are.
Integrity is what we really are.

JOHN MAXWELL

Every generation needs a new revolution.

THOMAS JEFFERSON

$$\Longrightarrow\!\!\bullet\!\!\Longleftarrow$$

If you're not doing something with your life, it doesn't matter how long it is.

PEACE CORPS COMMERCIAL

If your vision doesn't cost you something, it's a daydream.

JOHN MAXWELL

When you don't want to do something,
one excuse is as good as another.

———⟫◆⟪———

Ninety-nine percent of failures come
from people who have the habit
of making excuses.

GEORGE WASHINGTON CARVER

Our attitude at the beginning of a task will affect its outcome more than anything else.

JOHN MAXWELL

You can impress people at a distance,
but you can impact them only up close.

HOWARD HENDRICKS

Our strength is seen in the things we stand for;
our weakness is seen in the things we fall for.

THEODORE EPP

If people respect you but don't like
you, they won't stay with you.
If they like you but don't respect
you, they'll stay with you,
but they won't follow you.
To be an effective leader, you
must earn both from your people.

JOHN MAXWELL

One-fifth of the people are against
everything all the time.

ROBERT KENNEDY

I am only one, but I am one. I cannot do
everything, but I can do something. And that
which I can do, by the grace of God, I will do.

DWIGHT L. MOODY

Your attitude is the eye of your soul.
If your attitude is negative,
then you see things negatively.
If it's positive, then
you see things positively.

JOHN MAXWELL

We judge ourselves by what we feel capable of doing; others judge us by what we have done.

HENRY WADSWORTH LONGFELLOW

＝◆＝

It's right to be content with what you have, never with what you are.

You cannot go any higher
than your self-image.

JOHN MAXWELL

No reserve, no retreat, and no regrets.

BILL BORDON
MISSIONARY TO CHINA
WRITTEN ON HIS DEATH BED

—————⟩◆⟨—————

Never retreat in the face of difficulties.
Advance as conditions permit.
If conditions don't permit,
create those conditions.

A difficult crisis can be more readily endured
if we retain the conviction that our existence
holds a purpose— a cause to pursue,
a person to love, a goal to achieve.

JOHN MAXWELL

Before putting off until tomorrow something you can do today, study it closely. Maybe you can postpone it indefinitely.

Don't put off for tomorrow what you can do today, because if you enjoy it today, you can do it again tomorrow.

JAMES A. MICHENER

A procrastinator puts off until tomorrow the things he has already put off until today.

JOHN MAXWELL

Do what you can, with what you have,
where you are.

THEODORE ROOSEVELT

When you cease to make a
contribution, you begin to die.

ELEANOR ROOSEVELT

The true test of stewardship is not
what your money is doing for you
but what it's doing to you.

JOHN MAXWELL

Safe living generally makes for regrets later on.

⇒◈⇐

You miss 100 percent of
the shots you never take.

WAYNE GRETZKY

The greatest mistake we make is living
in constant fear that we will make one.

JOHN MAXWELL

Make no small plans,
for they have no capacity
to stir men's souls.

——◆——

The future belongs to people
who see possibilities
before they become obvious.

TED LEVITT

Problems are those things we see
when we take our eyes off the goal.

JOHN MAXWELL

I will go anywhere as long as it's forward.

DAVID LIVINGSTONE

The man who starts out going nowhere,
generally gets there.

DALE CARNEGIE

Vision adds value to everything.

JOHN MAXWELL

Opportunities are seldom labeled.

JOHN A. SHEDD

—⊰◆⊱—

The desire for safety stands against
every great and noble enterprise.

What I *perceive*...
determines what I *receive*...
which determines how I *achieve*.

JOHN MAXWELL

It takes less time to do a thing right
than to explain why you did it wrong.

HENRY WADSWORTH LONGFELLOW

—————◆—————

Between saying and doing,
many a pair of shoes
is worn out.

ITALIAN PROVERB

People do what people see.
They forget your words
but follow your footsteps.

JOHN MAXWELL

If you want to make enemies,
try to change something.

WOODROW WILSON

———◆———

Do not follow where the path may lead.
Follow God, instead, to where there is
no path and leave a trail.

Leading others takes courage.
Knowing the right decision is usually easy.
Making the right decision is hard.

JOHN MAXWELL

The hottest places in Hell are reserved for
those who in time of great moral crises
maintain their neutrality.

———⊰◆⊱———

Why not go out on a limb?
Isn't that where the fruit is?

FRANK SCULLY

Leading followers is fast and easy,
and it has little return;
leading leaders is slow and hard,
and it has a great return.

JOHN MAXWELL

People who never do any more than
they get paid for, never get paid for
any more than they do.

ELBERT HUBBARD

><><

People who live for themselves
are in a mighty small business.

Winners concentrate on winning;
losers concentrate on getting by.

JOHN MAXWELL

Keep away from people who belittle
your ambitions. Small people always do
that, but the really great make you feel
that you, too, can become great.

MARK TWAIN

Consider how hard it is to change yourself
and you'll understand what little chance
you have of trying to change others.

JACOB M. BRAUDE

Loving people precedes leading them. People don't care how much you know until they know how much you care.

JOHN MAXWELL

The difficulties of life are intended
to make us better—not bitter.

———◆———

Life doesn't do anything to you.
It only reveals your spirit.

Hurting people hurt other people. Once you learn this, it's easier to "turn the other cheek."

JOHN MAXWELL

Are you gonna get any better, or is this it?

BALTIMORE ORIOLES MANAGER
EARL WEAVER—TO AN UMPIRE

⟫◆⟪

A rut is a grave with
both ends knocked out.

If you need the people,
you can't lead the people.
A co-dependent relationship
seldom grows or moves forward.

JOHN MAXWELL

Men will never cast away their dearest
pleasures upon the drowsy request
of someone who does not even seem
to mean what he says.

⟫⟩◆⟨⟪

Don't ever be afraid to admit
you were wrong. It's like saying
you're wiser today
than you were yesterday.

Every change in human
attitude must come through internal
understanding and acceptance. Man is the
only known creature who can reshape
and remold himself by
altering his attitude.

JOHN MAXWELL

Time is neutral; but it can be made the ally of those who will seize it and use it to the full.

WINSTON CHURCHILL

———◆———

Essentially there are two actions in life.
Performance and excuses.
Make a decision as to which
you will accept for yourself.

STEPHEN BROWN

The leader's growth determines the people's growth.

JOHN MAXWELL

Great minds have purposes;
others have wishes.

WASHINGTON IRVING

Never give up, for that is just the place
and time that the tide will turn.

HARRIET BEECHER STOWE

It's lonely at the top . . . so you'd
better know why you're there.

JOHN MAXWELL

Excellence is the gradual result
of always striving to do better.

PAT RILEY

Excellence is the gradual result
of always striving to do better.

———◆———

A good heart is better than all
the heads in the world.

EDWARD BULWER-LYTTON

It's wonderful when the people
believe in their leader;
it's more wonderful when the
leader believes in the people.

JOHN MAXWELL

Only the person who has faith in himself
is able to be faithful to others.

ERICH FROMM

———◈———

Learning what you cannot do
is more important than
knowing what you can do.

LUCILLE BALL

Leadership functions on the basis of trust.
When trust is gone, the leader soon will be.

JOHN MAXWELL

When was the last time that you
did something for the first time?

———⟨◆⟩———

Ninety percent of the work done
in this country is done by people
who don't feel well.

THEODORE ROOSEVELT

Nothing is as hard as it looks;
everything is more rewarding than you
expect; and if anything can
go right it will and at the
best possible moment.

MAXWELL'S LAW

Difficulties mastered
are opportunities won.

WINSTON CHURCHILL

—◆—

Commitment in the face of conflict
produces character.

People buy into the leader *before*
they buy into the leader's vision.
If you want to lead,
you must sell yourself.

JOHN MAXWELL

Anyone who has made a mistake and doesn't correct it, is making another one.

———◆———

You never have to recover from a good start.

Admit your failures quickly and humbly.
The people already know when you've erred,
but they'll appreciate your right spirit.

JOHN MAXWELL

The harder you work,
the harder it is to surrender.

VINCE LOMBARDI

⟫◈⟪

Persistence is stubbornness with a purpose.

RICH DEVOS

Never take shortcuts . . . .
They don't pay off in the long run.

JOHN MAXWELL

One cannot leap a chasm in two jumps.

WINSTON CHURCHILL

———◆———

Read the best books first, or you may
not have a chance to read them at all.

HENRY DAVID THOREAU

Where there is no hope in the future, there is no power in the present.

JOHN MAXWELL

God never puts anyone in
a place too small to grow.

———◆———

Christians are supposed not merely to endure
change, nor even profit by it, but to cause it.

HARRY EMERSON FOSDICK

I teach what I know,
but I reproduce what I am.

JOHN MAXWELL

Your friends will
stretch your vision
or choke your dream.

———⊰◆⊱———

Look carefully at the closest
associations in your life,
for that is the direction
you are heading.

People are your only appreciable asset.

JOHN MAXWELL

Life is a lot like tennis—
the one who can serve
best seldom loses.

The measure of a life, after all
is not its duration but its donation.

CORRIE TEN BOOM

Leadership is servanthood.
Observance of this truth
keeps your motives pure
and protects you from ambition.
It also makes you like Jesus.

JOHN MAXWELL

When God measures man,
he puts the tape around
his heart, not his head.

—=◆=—

If you think you can, you can.
And if you think you can't,
you're right.

MARY KAY ASH

Problems are not your problems.
It's not what happens *to* you but
what happens *in* you that matters.

JOHN MAXWELL

Experience is knowing a lot of
things you shouldn't do.

WILLIAM KNUDSON

⇒◆⇐

The young man knows the rules, but
the old man knows the exceptions.

OLIVER WENDELL HOLMES

Most people are educated way
beyond their level of obedience.

JOHN MAXWELL

Progress always involves risks.
You can't steal second
and keep your foot on first.

FREDERICK WILCOX

All life is the management of risk,
not its elimination.

WALTER WRISTON

Timing is everything.
The right set-up will keep an organization
from having a wrong setback.

JOHN MAXWELL

The difference between what we do and what we are capable of doing would suffice to solve most of the world's problems.

MAHATMA GANDHI

—◄►◄—

If we did all the things we are capable of doing, we would literally astonish ourselves.

THOMAS EDISON

To lead others to do right
is wonderful. To do right
and then lead them is more
wonderful . . . and harder.

JOHN MAXWELL

A determined person is one who,
when they get to the end of their rope,
ties a knot and hangs on.

JOE L. GRIFFITH

———◆———

Above all, try something.

FRANKLIN D. ROOSEVELT

God chooses what we go through;
we choose how we go through it.

JOHN MAXWELL

Nobody gets to run the mill by
doing run-of-the-mill work.

THOMAS J. FRYE

———◆———

You have to give up to go up.

DAVID JEREMIAH

Respect is vital to a leader.
Without it, no one follows.
Title or position will not help it.
With it, everyone follows, and
title or position are not needed.

JOHN MAXWELL

I make progress by having people around me
who are smarter than I am—and listening
to them. And I assume that everyone
is smarter about something than I am.

HENRY KAISER

⥲◆⥲

Progress is a tide. If we stand still
we will surely be drowned.
To stay on the crest,
we have to keep moving.

HAROLD MAYFIELD

Those closest to the leader determine
his level of success or failure.
Mentoring potential leaders
insures the leader and the
organizationof reaching
their potential.

JOHN MAXWELL

My God-given talent is my ability to stick
with something longer than anyone else.

HERSCHEL WALKER
HEISMAN TROPHY WINNER

———◆———

A great man stands on God.

RALPH WALDO EMERSON

The gift is greater than the leader.
God's anointing upon our lives
points to His greatness, not ours.

JOHN MAXWELL

Never, never stop growing.
Plateaus should only be found
in geography books,
not in personal experience.

One who gains strength by
overcoming obstacles
possesses the only strength
which can overcome adversity.

ALBERT SCHWEITZER

Leading people is a
responsibility, not a perk.
To whomever much is given,
much is required.

JOHN MAXWELL

Life is 10 percent what you make it
and 90 percent how you take it.

IRVING BERLIN

To err is human . . . but when the eraser wears
out ahead of the pencil, you're overdoing it.

JERRY JENKINS

Jesus is my best friend.
At times I have failed people.
At times people have failed me.
Jesus never fails.

JOHN MAXWELL

There are a lot of ways to become a failure, but never taking a chance is the most successful.

———◆———

Life is like a taxi. The meter just keeps a-ticking whether you are getting somewhere or just standing still.

LOU ERICKSON

You are only an attitude away from success!

JOHN MAXWELL

Make sure the thing you're living
for is worth dying for.

CHARLES MAYES

———⟫◆⟪———

People will work 8 hours a day for pay,
10 hours a day for a good boss, and
24 hours a day for a good cause!

Success isn't accumulating
possessions, wealth, or power.
Success is obeying God. It means
having those closest to you love
and respect you the most.

JOHN MAXWELL

The chief way you and I
are disloyal to Christ
is when we make small what
He intended to make large.

STANLEY JONES

When someone puts a limit
on what you will do,
that person has put a limit
on what you *can* do.

See your people as they
could be, not as they are.

JOHN MAXWELL

Don't think much of a person
who is not wiser today
than he was yesterday.

———◆———

Most of the things worth doing
in the world had been declared
impossible before they were done.

LOUIS D. BRANDEIS

The next time you go looking for a book written by an expert, find out if the author's ever actually done what he's proposing.

JOHN MAXWELL

Most people spend more time planning
Christmas than they do planning their lives.

Very often a change of self is needed
more than a change of scene.

BENSON

The attitude of your people is
a reflection of *your* attitude.

JOHN MAXWELL

When the eagles are silent,
the parrots begin to jabber.

WINSTON CHURCHILL

Often a leader's greatest challenge is
dealing with the multitudes of people
oblivious to the obvious.

Pastors shouldn't preach another sermon
until the people they lead do what they've
been asked to do in the last one.

JOHN MAXWELL

World records are only borrowed.

SEBASTIAN COE
BRITISH MIDDLE-DISTANCE RUNNER

———◆———

If something has been done a particular way for 15 or 20 years, it's a pretty good sign, in these changing times, that it is being done the wrong way.

ELLIOT M. ESTES

The question is not,
"Are you going to fail?"
The question is,
"How are you going to
handle your failure?"

JOHN MAXWELL

If at first you do succeed,
try something harder.

Success in life comes not from holding a good
hand, but in playing a poor hand well.

DENIS WAITLEY AND REM L. WITT

124

Life is not a dress rehearsal.

JOHN MAXWELL

We are living in days of change.
My grandfather had a farm.
My father had a garden.
But I've got a can opener.

⬥

We cannot become what we need
to be by remaining what we are.

Get a life of your own.
Where's the joy in inheriting someone else's?

JOHN MAXWELL

If in the last few years you haven't discarded a major opinion or acquired a new one, check your pulse. You may be dead.

GELETT BURGESS

Any business or industry that pays equal rewards to its goof-offs and its eager-beavers sooner or later will find itself with more goof-offs than eager-beavers.

MIKE DELANEY

"Average" has become so bad that
a person can just show up to go to
the head of the class.

JOHN MAXWELL

Most people are more comfortable with
old problems than with new solutions.

Be willing to give up all that you now
are to be all that you can become.

Growth is a process.
Death may be automatic,
but growth is not.

JOHN MAXWELL

We know what happens to people who stay in the middle of the road; they get run over.

ANEURIN BEVAN

———⬦———

Deliberation is the work of many men.
Action, of one alone.

CHARLES deGAULLE

If you keep doing what you've always done,
you'll always get what you've always gotten.

JOHN MAXWELL

The average person goes to his grave
with his music still in him.

OLIVER WENDELL HOLMES

———◆———

Most of us must learn a great deal every day
in order to keep ahead of what we forget.

FRANK A. CLARK

You cannot overestimate the unimportance
of practically everything.

JOHN MAXWELL

All accomplishment comes
from daring to begin.

———◆———

Eighty percent of success is showing up.

WOODY ALLEN

Many people go far in life because
someone else thought they could.

JOHN MAXWELL

If you're looking for a big opportunity,
seek out a big problem.

———◆———

The fewer the words, the better the prayer.

MARTIN LUTHER

If you want to help others,
don't just know your faith—
show your faith.

JOHN MAXWELL

No man ever listened himself out of a job.

CALVIN COOLIDGE

Everyone must row with the oars he has.

ENGLISH PROVERB

Circumstances do not make you what you are
. . . they reveal what you are!

JOHN MAXWELL

Walk so close to God that you
leave no room for the devil.

⟹◆⟸

If you don't do your homework,
you won't make your free throws.

LARRY BIRD

Are you feeling far from God?
Guess who moved?

JOHN MAXWELL

He who never walks except
where he sees other men's tracks
will make no discoveries.

———◆———

If your horse is dead,
for goodness sake—dismount!

EDDY KETCHURSID

To go nowhere, follow the crowd.

JOHN MAXWELL

Restlessness is discontent—and
discontent is the first necessity of progress.
Show me a thoroughly satisfied man—
and I will show you a failure.

THOMAS EDISON

Inspiration without perspiration is a daydream;
perspiration without inspiration is a nightmare.

Any time you let up, expect a letdown.

JOHN MAXWELL

The reasonable man adapts himself to the world; the unreasonable one persists in trying to adapt the world to himself. Therefore all progress depends on the unreasonable man.

GEORGE BERNARD SHAW

The world is moving so fast these days that the man who says it can't be done is generally interrupted by someone doing it.

ELBERT HUBBARD

People are like rubber bands:
They must be stretched
to be effective.

JOHN MAXWELL

The reason so many people never get anywhere in life is because, when opportunity knocks, they are out in the backyard looking for four-leaf clovers.

WALTER P. CHRYSLER

⟞◆⟝

Everything comes to him who hustles while he waits.

THOMAS EDISON

Leadership development is a
life-time journey— not a weekend trip.

JOHN MAXWELL

You have never tested God's resources
until you have attempted the impossible.

Achievers are not only persistent, they are also
hard workers who believe in themselves.

TIMOTHY L. GRIFFITH

Whiners achieve
only when they feel like it.
Winners achieve
even when they don't.

JOHN MAXWELL

A Thoroughbred horse never
looks at the other horses.
It just concentrates on running
the fastest race it can.

HENRY FONDA

⋙◆⋘

The farsighted tend to
get blindsided by the
nearsighted.

Those who follow the crowd
will never be followed by a crowd.

JOHN MAXWELL

If we study the giants, we
are less apt to be pygmies.

—◆—

You must have long-range goals to keep you
from being frustrated by short-range failures.

CHARLES C. NOBLE

Decisions are made in a moment, but growth comes from daily discipline.

JOHN MAXWELL

About John Maxwell

John C. Maxwell is the founder of INJOY, a San Diego-based Christian leadership organization dedicated to helping leaders reach their potential in ministry, business, and the family.

For 26 years he pastored churches, including one of America's largest for 14 years as its senior pastor. A popular speaker, John offers ongoing leadership instruction through the INJOY Life Club, a monthly tape service. He speaks nationally and internationally on subjects such as leadership, personal growth, attitude, Christian living, and church growth.

John is the author of over a dozen books published by Focus on the Family, Thomas Nelson, Victor Books and Honor Books.

How would you like to join the Club...the INJOY Life Club! By becoming a member, you'll receive a new motivational tape by Dr. John C. Maxwell each month. Call 1-800-333-6506 to find out how you can join the INJOY Life Club.

INJOY is a non-denominational Christian leadership institute founded in 1984 by Dr. John C. Maxwell. INJOY is committed to increasing the leadership effectiveness of people in ministry, business, and the family. INJOY offers a wide variety of training seminars, books, videos, and audio cassettes designed to increase your ability to influence and lead others. For more information concerning John C. Maxwell or INJOY write or call:

INJOY
5295 Triangle Parkway
Norcross, Georgia 30092
1-800-333-6506

Additional copies of this book or the following
titles by John C. Maxwell are available from
Honor Books or your local bookstore:

Leadership 101

*You Can't Be a Smart Cookie if
You Have a Crummy Attitude*

*People Power: Life's Little
Lessons on Relationships*

Tulsa, Oklahoma